# THE ULTI___ GUIDE TO FISHING FUN!

## MORE JOKES, CARTOONS, TIPS, TRIVIA, AND LAUGHS THAN YOU CAN SHAKE A POLE AT!

BY STEVE LEE

Cover Art By
omkumis @ Fiverr

2022 Morning Dew Entertainment

Dedicated to David Lee,
who taught me how much someone can love the world of fishing.

# TABLE OF CONTENTS

"Okay, maybe it only weighed two hundred pounds."

# Fishlore & More

# Late winter & early spring crankbait tips

- Focus on the current breaks. The water gets dirtier as the water levels rise in late winter and early spring. Bass are better positioned in predictable areas such eddies behind boulders, slack water behind points, and other current deflection when the water is rising.

- Use balsa finesse crankbaits. Many fishermen start off with smaller crankbaits with a softer action and have more success. Many typically start by casting a balsa flat-sided crankbait at shallow water, making sure to make contact with the cover as you reel in the bait. Similar to jerkbaits, the best baits have a gradual rise that keeps them in the striking zone for longer. This might be crucial for gaining strikes in cold water.

- Always maintain bottom contact. Bass with a modern influence hugs the ground and any important cover components tightly. The strike window is smaller in cold, murky water, so be sure to place and maintain your bait there.

- Crankbaits with neutral buoyancy or gradual rise qualities, as noted above, aid in keeping the lure where it matters. Include pauses, pulls, and interactions with the cover and structure as the bait rams into it and careens over it.

- Have a number of crankbaits available. Try varying running depths to locate various fish populations. To work nearby edges and flats, try following up a shallow cranking pass with a deeper diver. A 4- to 6-foot diving bait can only sustain easy bottom contact for a short period of time whereas an 8- to 10-foot diver works a very fruitful depth zone. In conclusion, be prepared with subtle shallow- and mid-depth baits.

- Set up a light rod. Because bass frequently skin hook in cold water, many pros choose a light power rod with a slower taper to prevent hook tearing. The best straight fluorocarbon for reaching maximum running depth is in the 10- to 12-pound test range.

But officer, I'm sure that I'm not over the weight limit.

It was two days into their honeymoon when Jane realized that Jim was using their time away as an excuse for an exotic fishing trip.

The day the worms fought back.

# Fish Tales

**The fisherman vs The Sucker. Who will win?**

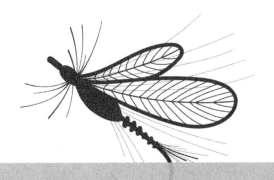

# Pro Tip

Be sure to "match the hatch" when selecting your type and size of flies. You want to imitate the size of the insects that are currently hatching. During the hatch, fish become highly picky, and size is the most important determining factor.

This was the day that Mary Jane's goal to outfish the boys came back to bite her.

How about we tell the employees that we are going to a three-day ethics seminar, and instead, we go fishing?

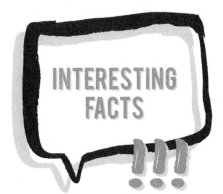

INTERESTING FACTS

Muskies and pike enjoy hiding in cold water. As a result, take caution to first check the water's temperature before casting your rod. Muskies usually enjoy swimming in water that is between 60 and 70 degrees Fahrenheit. Pike, on the other hand, favors waters that are 50 to 55 degrees.

# Pro Tip

When you are trolling, make sure that your lures appear to swim in a lifelike manner. Try accelerating a little bit if they appear lethargic.

On the other hand, ease back on the throttle if the lures appear spastic and unnatural in how they appear to swim. The fish can tell the difference, and it will make a difference in how many fish you catch.

# I DON'T ALWAYS TELL MY SECRET FISHING SPOTS, BUT WHEN I DO...

## I LIE

# Which fly rod weight is best?

Number 5-weight fly rods are typically considered the best all-around option for anglers. 5-weight fly rods can manage delicate casts in alpine streams and 20-inch trout in rivers and lakes.

The 5-weight may be an excellent all-around pick for most fishermen, but perhaps not for you.

How do you know which fly rod weight to use?

Fly rod weight refers to what size fishing line you can use. A 5-weight fly rod is meant for a 5-weight line. Every fly rod lets you increase or reduce the fly line by one step. A 5-weight rod can employ a 4-, 5-, or 6-weight line. So with the three line weights, you can fish small mountain streams or larger rivers with hard-fighting trout. That's why a 5-weight is a fantastic all-around pick.

The size and species of fish you'll be casting at will help you choose the optimal all-around fly rod weight.

If you fish primarily in small alpine streams and creeks, a 5-weight may be too hefty. If you're going to fight 10 to 12" brook trout all day, get a 4-weight or 3-weight fly rod. The lighter weight will help you finesse the fish and improve your experience.

If you are making long casts and fighting larger fish in bigger rivers, a 6-weight may be a better choice for you. The reality is that you need to decide what type of fishing you are planning, and that will help you pick the rod size.

FRED FINALLY UNDERSTOOD WHY YOU READ THE SIGNS BEFORE YOU FISH.

GOVERNMENT REGULATED FISH

# Pro Tip

Choose the right fishing line for the approximate weight of fish you are trying to catch. i.e.- 4-pound test for trout, 30-pound test for tuna. If you are new to fishing, ask someone at a Pro Shop what they consider best for your fishing style and type of fish you are going after.

You don't have to be crazy to fish with us.
We can teach you.

GOD grant me the SERENITY

to accept
the SIZE of the fish I catch,
the COURAGE not to FIB about it
and the WISDOM to know that
NO ONE would BELIEVE me anyway

18

# BOOMER'S WORLD

BOOMER DECIDED THAT HE WANTED TO LEARN TO FISH.

THIS COULD BE FUN.

UNTIL HE NEARLY BECAME A SHISH KABOB FOR A SWORDFISH...

AND THE FAVORITE LURE FOR ALL THE LAKE FISH!

THEN CAME THE DAY HE WAS NOODLING FOR CATFISH AND HE NEARLY LOST HIS ARM...

AND WHEN HE WAS BASS FISHING IN THE EVERGLADES AND NEARLY BECAME GATOR FOOD.

IT WAS ON THE DAY HE CAUGHT HIS FIRST TROPHY FISH THAT HE UNDERSTOOD THE LOVE OF FISHING

THEN CAME THE DAY WITH THE SEA MONSTER.

THIS IS THE BEST!

© 2022 S LEE

# KAYAK FISHING

KAYAK FISHING

Kayak fishing takes a long time to learn how to do well. The time it takes to learn how to fish from a kayak can be frustrating and sometimes takes years. Having an old-timer help, you is about as close as you can get to a shortcut. It's always best to have an experienced kayaker take the first-timer under his/her wing and let the newbie go fishing with them in a kayak.

Kayak fishing requires the angler to learn how to steady the kayak while he/she attempts to paddle through the waters; this is a necessary component of the entire procedure. So here are a couple of suggestions for those who are interested in learning more about kayak fishing:

# 1. Put safety first.

As with any activity, it is essential that a person adopts some safety precautions and do some checking before getting starting. The angler should always be aware of the weather, the tide, and other kayaking-related safety issues. It is wise to let someone know your general location before entering the water.

# 2. Always keep the hatches closed

When fishing from a kayak, it is advisable to keep the hatches closed. Keeping the hatches closed prevents loss of your tackle as well as keeping water from entering the kayak.

# 3. Plan Ahead

Try to keep the kayak stable while dealing with catching larger fish; it is advisable to have an anchor.

Some people say that a bad day of fishing is still better than a good day at work. I say, a bad day of fishing is the perfect day to catch a beer.

# Pro Tip

Use brightly colored baits when fishing in muddy water and use more subtle colors when you're in clear water.

**DID YOU KNOW?**

Even the smallest catfish has more than 250,000 taste buds. But that's only the tip of the sensory iceberg when it comes to catfish.

The catfish has a good sense of smell, too. Some compounds can be smelled by catfish at a level of one part per 10 billion parts of water.

Inside the catfish's nostrils, water flows over folds of very sensitive tissue, which lets the fish sense certain things in its environment. The number of these folds seems to have something to do with how strong the smell is.

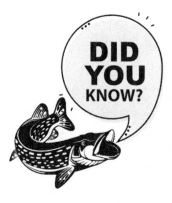

**DID YOU KNOW?**

American fishermen spend $7.4 billion on just fishing gear. Rod, reel, lines, bait, and hooks are all included in that. Assuming there are 60 million anglers in the United States, that means each one spends $120 a year on equipment. And when you consider that lines, hooks, bait, and lures receive the lion's share of this money, that's some serious fishing.

# Pro Tip

The best times for catching fish are when they are most naturally active. Fish are influenced by the Sun, Moon, tides, and weather.
Fish tend to feed more at sunrise and sunset. The "morning rise" (just after sun-up) and the "evening rise" (an hour before and after sundown. They also feed when there is a slight rain or drizzle. When saltwater fishing, going during a full moon when tides are higher than average is also a good time. Also, about an hour before and after high tides and an hour before and after low tides are good times to cast your line.

"Excuse me, but do I go to your local market
and steal all the snacks?"

"Whoever loses is my dinner."

# Tips To Improve Underwater Spearfishing

Spear Fishing

Before you ever enter the water, you need to be ready. To succeed, you need to use the appropriate equipment and use a spearfishing strategy that is appropriate for the region where you are fishing.

- First, become comfortable in the water. Getting aggressive in the water will scare off your prey, so calm down. Relax, and move through the water as if you were supposed to be there.

- Learn everything you can about the locale where you will be diving. Each Spearo (nickname of an avid spear fisher-person) will have unique experiences and recommendations.

Pay attention, and don't be shy about asking questions. Log your dives and record what worked and didn't work at each diving site.

- Learn the tides and weather conditions for each of your fishing spots.

- Avoid pursuing fish. Although you are a predator in the water, you are not in your natural element. Be calm and you will have much better luck.

- Most importantly, use your gun with caution. A speargun is a dangerous weapon. Safety should always be engaged while hunting, and you should never, ever point your weapon towards someone else.

What's the difference between a piano and a fish? You can tune a piano but you can't tuna fish!

# Pro Tip

You should set your reel's drag at a number that is somewhere between 1/4 to 1/3 of your line's breaking strength.

DID YOU KNOW?

Ever ponder the origin of the term "anglers"? It derives from the word "angle," which means "hook," in Old English. Therefore, persons who fish with hook and line are referred to as anglers. So a person who catches a fish using any other method is not an angler.

THERE'S A SUCKER BORN EVERY MINUTE...ESPECIALLY WHEN IT COMES TO FISHERMEN.

Fred and Ethel found that a couple that fishes together stays together--as long as they fish from opposite ends of the boat.

While there is no reason for fish to swim backward, the majority of them can if necessary. Sharks, however, cannot. Their stiff fins do not bend. As a result, they cannot swim backwards or abruptly cease swimming.

# Ice Fishing Safety

Typically, the greatest ice fishing will be available when the season's first safe ice forms. The fish are hungry, haven't learned what to be aware of by the onslaught of ice fisherman who will soon be tormenting them, and they have been relatively unmolested by anglers for the time when the ice is beginning to form.

Early season ice fishing might potentially be hazardous since the ice has not had time to become thick enough. As a general guideline, aim for a minimum of 4 inches of solid ice (see chart below). Always check the thickness of the ice as you walk away from the beach, and make sure you are wearing a life jacket or flotation device. Never go out on the ice by yourself, and always have a thick rope in your possession. Stay away from regions where a stream or brook flows nearby, as well as from trees or huge branches that extend into the lake, as these features will absorb heat from the sun and damage the ice.

Different bodies of water will freeze at varying rates of speed. This is significant. For example, a town reservoir may not have safe ice even if you see someone skating on a nearby slough.

Any body of water's south side of a hill will usually freeze more quickly than its north side since it gets less sunshine. Larger bodies of water take longer to freeze than small, shallow ones. Ice often builds up on a pond at a pace of roughly 1/2 inch each day during a good freeze. So there should be some safe ice to be found if you have a whole week with temperatures below freezing.

## ICE THICKNESS CHART

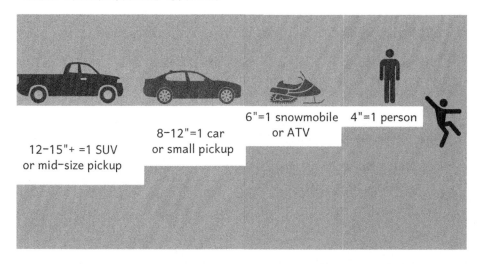

12-15"+ =1 SUV
or mid-size pickup

8-12"=1 car
or small pickup

6"=1 snowmobile
or ATV

4"=1 person

## Did You Know?

Ice fishing is the fourth most popular winter pastime in the state of Wisconsin, after ice skating, snowmobiling, and sledding respectively.

STOP DRILLING!
THERE'S NO FISH THERE.
THANKS.
DUDE, THERE'S NO FISH THERE EITHER.
WHATEVER.
WHAT DON'T YOU UNDERSTAND?
THERE'S NO FISH HERE.
IS THAT YOU GOD?
NO, BUT I OWN THIS SKATING RINK!

# Pro Tip

Minnows are the most preferred bait for anglers fishing for walleye. Shiner and flathead minnows work well. When targeting larger fish, 4-6" shiners will weed through lesser fish and get you 25"+ Walleye.

There comes a time when you have to take a step back from life's insanity and say, "to hell with it all, I'm going fishing."

# Summer Steelhead vs Winter Steelhead

Female fish from the summer run enter the freshwater system carrying immature eggs. Winter steelhead, on the other hand, arrive in river systems fully developed sexually and are prepared to spawn. Summer fish may stay in the freshwater system for much of the year, whereas winter fish may only spend a matter of days in the river system.

## Summer Steelhead Strategies

- The strategies are a little bit different for each because of the variances between the two. Steelhead that migrates during the summer arrives in Washington and Oregon in the late spring. In some areas, you can venture outside and begin angling as early as May. Typically the lower clear water leads the angler to use smaller, more traditional fly patterns. Longer rods (12–14 feet) work better for casting smaller flies, along with longer Scandi lines for delicate presentations and longer leads, which enhance the casting experience.

- Fish in the summer are more aggressive and will travel further to catch a swung fly, so you may move swiftly through a run while looking for these active fish by moving 8 to 10 feet between throws. Summer steelhead catches can be some of the most thrilling fly-fishing experiences an angler can enjoy.

## Winter Steelhead Techniques

- Steelhead fishing in the winter is a very different sport. Many winter fish move up little coastal streams to spawn. Winter weather, including rain, snow, icy roads, and high river flows, keeps many the more timid anglers indoors. Skagit lines are necessary to offer larger profile flies (like intruders) and a sink tip to break surface tension and present to fish at a lower level in the water column. Shorter rods (10-11.5'), with shorter Skagit heads and leads are needed for winter fly fishing in order to swing the fly down and over the tailout to the waiting fish.

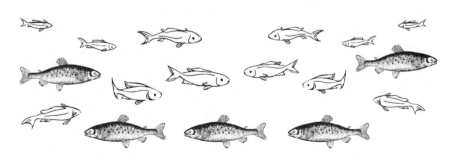

# The best day of my life!

I caught a 27-pound grouper on a 12-lb test!

INTERESTING FACTS

Color dissipates the deeper it goes under water. The first color that fades under water is red. Red disappears in as little as 15 feet. Thus, red is an excellent line color if you are fishing in deep water since your bait will look more realistic, and the line will appear invisible to fish the deeper it goes. Another interesting fact is that Sockeye Salmon are the only fish that can see red.

# Walley Love Leeches

Leeches are among the best live baits to use for walleye fishing. Yes, those disgusting little bloodsuckers are excellent fish bait.

However, you might be thinking, "How do I catch leeches?" While some states allow you to purchase them from bait vendors, many regions require you to gather your own. They can be caught using this long-forgotten technique, and you can find them in ponds with lots of cattails or lily pads.

Put a sizable chunk of fresh beef liver inside a burlap sack that has several dozen knife-punched holes in it. Throw the sack into shallow water after tying off the end with a rope. The bloody liver will be accessible to leeches through the perforations and frayed fabric; when you return and draw it in, bingo! You have some fish bait.

# Pro Tip

If it's hot outside, fish deeper. As the temperature outside climbs, fish retreat to deeper, cooler water. During twilight and dawn, fish feed in shallower water, some more shallow than others. You should research the fish you want to catch.

**DID YOU KNOW?** Fish have sleep-like intervals in which their responsiveness to stimuli is reduced, their physical activity is slowed, and their metabolism is reduced, but they do not experience the same changes in brain waves as people do when they sleep.

Happiness can't be bought, but fishing gear can, and that's nearly the same thing.

Catfish can hear effectively despite having no apparent ears. Catfish are water-dense, thus they don't need external ears. Sound waves in water pass through a catfish. Sound waves vibrate a fish's swim bladder. This intensifies sound waves, which reach inner ear bones (otoliths). The otoliths vibrate, bending hairlike projections on the cells below them. These nerves send sound to the brain.

# A Few Techniques for Fishing Yellowtail

Bait and lures are effective methods for catching Yellowfin tuna. Many methods will be effective. Topwater tactics can be employed because these tuna frequently eat close to the surface. Since Yellowtail have relatively good vision, you might want to try a fluorocarbon leader to lessen visibility.

Chumming is frequently successful whether used as bait or as a lure while fishing for all types of tuna, including Yellowfin. You can chum with either live or cut bait chunks. This encourages the fish to congregate near the boat.

## Lures for Yellowfin Tuna

- Try tuna feathers, cedar plugs, and plastic skirted trolling lures when trolling. Rapala-style plugs also work. Because it can be trolled quickly, the Halco Max makes a good trolling plug. When in doubt, the colors blue, white, and green are frequently appropriate choices. Single or double hooks are less prone to bend or shake. The cedar plugs don't seem like much, but they certainly do the job.

- If you find a group of fish that are feeding, you can throw lures at them. Poppers are a good way to catch them. Both conventional chugger lures were retrieved in a pattern of "pop-pop-pause." A consistent retrieve with a ranger-style bait skipping over the surface frequently produces fish. Yo-Zuri Sashimi Bull is arguably one of the very best all-around poppers for tuna. It can be popped slowly or quickly over the top, and the colors are stunning. Since tuna have good eyesight, a quicker retrieve with them is often a good practice, but when they're really hungry, they will sometimes bite lures that are just sitting there.

- A stickbait that has recently gained popularity is the Shimano Orca. It is swiftly worked close to the surface.

- And finally, when the fish are deep, metal jigs in blue and metallic colors frequently work effectively.

All fishermen are liars, except you and me...
**And I'm not sure about you.**

# Best Pro Tip

If you're going to lie, at least make it believable.

**Before he knew it,
Schmidty had invented lacrosse.**

# Riverboat Safety Tips

River safety is always important. Here are a few tips that could save your life.

- Tell someone where you're going, when you plan to get back and their contact information in case you have an emergency.
- It should go without saying, but many an angler has died by avoiding this one simple rule. Never run a river alone. Make sure your boating and whitewater skills are appropriate for the river and the circumstances.
- When you are in or near the river, always wear a Personal Flotation Device (PFD) that is correctly fitted.

- Understand your capabilities for self-rescue and swimmer rescue in whitewater rivers. Know when to look for an eddy and how to use it.
- Be ready for weather extremes, especially the cold. Understand the risks of hypothermia and how to treat it. Recognize the early warning signs and symptoms of dehydration and heat exhaustion.
- Wearing protective footwear and appropriate apparel can lessen the risk of harm.
- Always carry a first aid kit in your boat, and be familiar with its use. CPR and medical aid duties should be learned or reviewed.
- Run rapids only if there is a clear passage through them. After the winter and spring floods, be on the lookout for fresh obstacles.
- Before you enter a set of rapids, give the boat in front of you time to pass through it. In the event that the leading boat gets caught in the rapids, you have a way to get around it and prevent a double calamity.
- If you are in waters that you don't know, or if the water depths have changed due to runoff, or some other reason. It is wise to stop and scout downstream if you're in doubt. If you have any remaining doubts? Portage may be the best and safest solution.

Education is important, but fishing is more importanter!

# A Few Grubby Tips for Trout

Here's a tip you may not have considered for catching trout. Bee moth larvae are among the best baits for trout. They are regularly offered for sale at docks and bait shops under the name "wax worms".

Three or four of these waxy-colored grubs should be placed on a fine-wire hook, with the ends left to dangle enticingly. A small cork float can be placed on your line directly above the hook, this helps keep the wax worms more buoyant so the fish can see them.

Although few modern anglers employ them, many older anglers still use grasshoppers and crickets, which often proves to make excellent trout bait. Put one on a thin-wired hook and fish it like a fly on top. Avoid weight and use a light line. Send it out. Wriggle it a little, and then wait for the fun.

 It says here that Waxworms are considered a pest by beekeepers because they eat honey and beeswax. Well, who doesn't like honey?

# Organizing Your Tackle Box

You'll be more prepared and equipped to rerig your lines quickly when you know how to organize a tackle box using a strategy that is based on the techniques you use and the species you target.

However, make sure you have the appropriate tackle box or bag for the type of fishing you enjoy before thinking about how to organize a tackle box. Consider a backpack-style tackle bag, for instance, if you're learning how to fish from a bank or shoreline so that you have more free hands for holding fishing rods. If you fish from a boat or kayak, opt for a waterproof tackle box with transparent trays.

Following a few basic steps will help you organize your tackle box, tackle bag, or backpack-style bag.

- Grouping gear for a particular species is a basic fishing tackle storage strategy. Keep all your largemouth crankbaits in one tray. Labeling each tray helps. You can immediately grab bass lures by labeling them "largemouth bass – crankbaits."

- Adjustable dividers in tackle trays can help you maximize storage space.
- Separate the soft plastic baits. Leave soft plastic baits in their original packaging if feasible. Keep bait shapes with a soft binder. Mixing delicate plastic baits can melt or bleed. Find a fishing tackle tutorial or video on storing soft plastic baits for additional information.
- Use smaller trays for your hooks and tackle. Hooks, weights, floats, and other small terminal gear should be stored in little trays or compartments.
- Store pliers and larger items in front pockets. Store line cutters and de-hookers in front pockets or huge compartments.
- Keep your various line options in the side pockets. Keep extra fishing line spools in side pockets or a smaller backpack.

These simple organization techniques will make your life easier when you are out on the water.

# Museum wall for Catch & Release Anglers ~~Liars~~

A FISHERMAN THAT SAYS, "JUST ONE MORE CAST"
IS THE SAME AS A WOMAN IN A STORE SAYING, "JUST FIVE MORE MINUTES."

Tides affect fishing because they move water. When current or water movement increases, fish are easier to catch because the moving water increases the activity of marine organisms they naturally feed on.

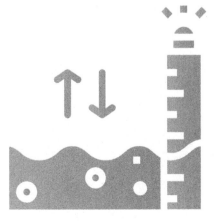

# Forget Prince Charming,
## I just want a man to take me fishing.

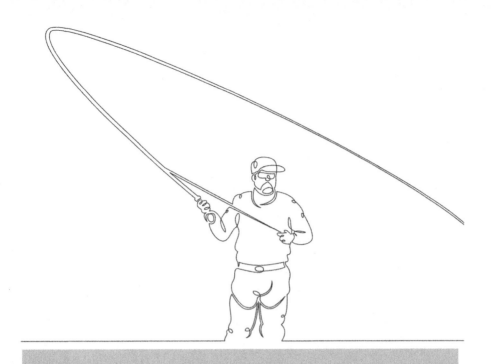

# Interesting Tips for Catching Bluegill

Here's a tip that you won't believe until you try it. Once it's worked for you, it will make you a believer. As crazy as it sounds, put a slice of banana peel into your cricket cage a day or two before you go out. The banana peel gives the crickets some additional aroma that bluegills love.

Mussels and snails also make excellent bait for bluegills and other panfish. FYI, catfish also love them.

When you get the snails and/or mussels, put them in a container with some water. Break open the snails before putting them on your hook for fishing. As for the mussels, use a knife to split open shell and then slice the meat into. pieces before putting them on your hook.

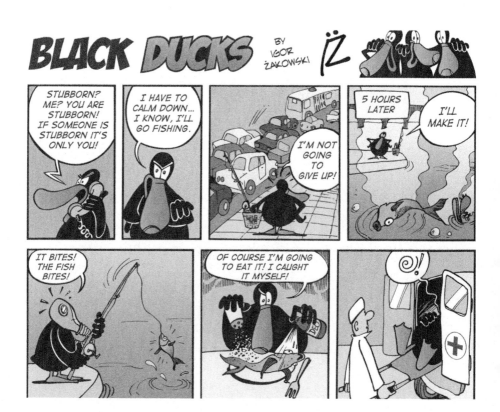

Sometimes you have to reel in a few failures
before you catch success.

# Pro Tip

Your health could be put at risk if you consume fish from contaminated waters. Mercury, dioxins, polychlorinated biphenyls (PCBs), and pesticide residues are the contaminants of greatest concern. Check for local fish advisories to find fish that are safe to eat.

# Did You Know?

Catfish rigs vary by method. The Carolina Rig is a popular catfish rig. This rig can be used for boat or bank fishing. Santee Rig is another effective catfish rig.

Welcome to our campfire, where after a day of fishing, we roast marshmallows-- and our friends.

Harold was always a
sucker for a pretty face.

Definition of a angler: A Jerk who spends all his money on "fishing stuff" and then sits in an overpriced boat all day waiting for another jerk to yank his line.

I'm so mad at my husband. He said that a woman's pain is so extreme during labor that she can ALMOST IMAGINE what a man feels when a fish gets away!

# *Pro Tip*

Here's how to make your wife happy when you arrange to go out on a big fishing trip that she may not appreciate. First and foremost, prioritize her needs. Otherwise, she feels like she's an afterthought. If you have the money, let her go shopping while you fish. That way she gets a fun trip just like you. Also, make sure she feels appreciated and can also get some relaxation time. Consider giving her a spa day, massage, some chocolates, or something else that she would like.

# That is just Crazy!

The largest freshwater fish is considered to be the sturgeon. The 27 different species of sturgeon make up the Acipenseridae family.

They are one of the few dinosaur-era creatures still in existence. The earliest sturgeon fossils come from the Late Cretaceous period and are related to earlier acipenseriform fish that lived between 174 and 201 million years ago in the Early Jurassic.

Sturgeons are a long-living and late-maturing type of fish that stand out for having features like a heterocercal caudal fin that resembles a shark's and an elongated, spindle-like body that is smooth-skinned, scaleless, and protected by five lateral rows of bone plates known as scutes. Several species of sturgeon have the potential to reach lengths of 7–12 ft in length and weigh up to 2,000 pounds.

A female beluga sturgeon that was caught in the Volga Delta, Russia in 1827 and measured 23' 7" long and weighed a whopping 3,463 pounds, becoming the largest sturgeon ever recorded.

How would like to reel in that big mama? That would be a great fish story without even having to lie!

# Picking A Fishing Guide

1. Communicate openly. You must give the guide all the necessary information to determine the finest fishing trip for you. Always tell the guide how much fishing experience you have. Be honest—don't oversell your skill level. This will enable them give you time-saving suggestions.

2. Ask friends and other anglers you know and trust whom they recommend. Ask about their experiences, what to do, and what to look for in a guide. They may also recommend useful guides they've used.

3. Check Guides Out Online. The Internet has many places where you can get local guides. You can send remarks and queries about the website, and they may help you. Sites like tripadvisor.com often provide such recommendations with customer reviews.

4. Verify your guide's license. Many states and countries require professional guides to be licensed. Knowing that your guide is legal is preferable. A licensed guide may be trusted for integrity and honesty. Ask the guide for their name and phone number, including state licensing.

5. Determine what you're paying for and how long the trip will last. You need this information to arrange your fishing excursion and bring items not covered by your payment. Some packages include lodging, while others do not. Asking about what is included will help you determine if the services are worth the money.

6. Get to know the guide that you are considering. Determine if your guide is compatible with you. You'll waste time and money otherwise. If you and your fishing guide don't get along, the trip could be ruined. Before starting your trip, call the guide to break the ice; it will make you both comfortable on your excursion.

7. Ask how long the guide has been operating. This will help you assess the guide's experience. Choose an experienced guide. They have helpful skills and instructional strategies.

I'm just another social drinker with a fishing problem.

# Pro Tip

Use baits or lures that can be worked on the bottom near ledges or drop-offs while lake fishing for largemouth bass. You should definitely consider giving soft-plastic worms, lizards, and jerkbaits a try.

THERE AREN'T A LOT OF THINGS
I ENJOY MORE THAN FISHING,
BUT ONE OF THEM IS...

WAIT, THERE'S NOTHING I LIKE MORE
THAN FISHING.

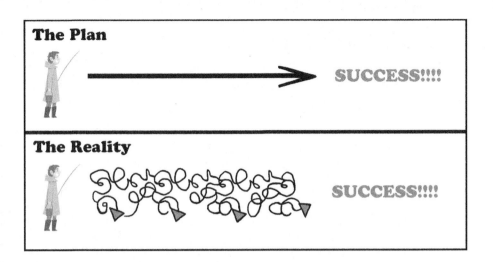

WHAT, YOU'VE NEVER HEARD OF PICKLED HERRRING?

# Pro Tip

If you are planning a fishing trip with children, always have snacks and other activities available for them. A child's attention span is often short. The key is to plan your trip properly so that you and the child can have fun. If they are having fun, it will make your day much better.

In that brief instant, Wormy understood that he was the bottom of the food chain.

PICKING THE RIGHT FISHING HOLE IS A PRIMARY RULE IN FISHING.

DID YOU KNOW?

Fish communicate with one another via a range of low-pitched sounds. They boom, hiss, whistle, creak, screech, wail, moan, grunt, croak, and so on. They gnash their teeth and rattle their bones. Fish don't have voice cords, though; they create noise with other parts of their bodies, such as by vibrating their muscles against their swim bladder.

# Pro Tip

When purchasing worms, request a paper bag and then store them in the shade with a couple of ice cubes. Your worms will stay cool and avoid drying out all day long in a brown bag.

# Work To ~~Live~~

## ~~LIVE TO WORK~~

### Live Fish

A day without fishing probably won't kill ya...but why chance it?

# Pro Tip

Depending on the month, different bugs and animals hatch in ponds and lakes. If you are unsure about the current hatch, check with a local Pro Shop and find out before you go. Also, depending on the region you are fishing in, try different things, like lures that look like shad, frogs, or grubs. Again, the local pros will know what works best.

**DID YOU KNOW?** Although minnows do not have true teeth, in order to digest their food, they use specialized teeth called pharyngeal teeth to mash it up against a plate-like structure that is found in the back of their throat.

TODAYS FORECAST, BEER WITH CHANCE OF FISHING.

# Pro Tip

When beginning as an ice fisher, use "tip-up" ice traps or a jigging rod to deploy bait through a hole in the ice. Most ice fishermen set out all their tip-ups and jig if they find a hot hole. First-time ice fishers should invest in tip-ups.

# Pro Tip

Check the label before spraying bug repellent on clothing. Spray DEET repellents on the outside of garments, pants, hats, and socks. It won't harm cotton, wool, or nylon, but beware of using it on leather.

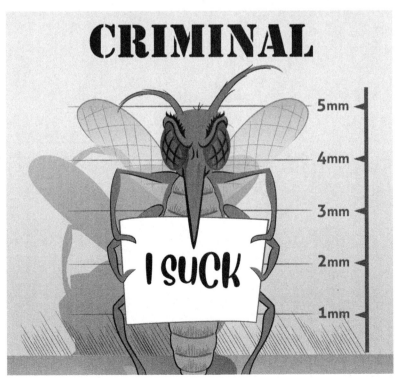

# Pro Tip

When it comes to catching swordfish at night, dead squid is the most effective form of bait. If you cut open the stomach of practically every swordfish, you will almost certainly discover that its stomach will be stuffed with squid. Many swordfishers favor using dried-out squid between 8 and 14 inches.

Work is for people who aren't smart enough to fish.

## Pro Tip

The most effective methods for deep sea fishing involve trolling with either natural or artificial baits. When bottom fishing, it might be helpful to use fishing lures such as huge jigs or heavy-duty rigs to lower your baits to a greater depth.

# A FISHY QUIZ

1. What's the world's healthiest fish to eat?
2. What is the biggest fish in the world?
3. What is a lumpsucker?
4. Some spearfishing masks have dark mirror glass. Why is this?
5. What are family groups of Dolphins called?
6. A soft-hackle nymph fly has just hooked one of the types of fish that are commonly caught using flies. What kind of fish would this be?
7. What three types of fish have the fewest calories?
8. What do you call a group of fish?
9. What is jerkbait lure?
10. What bait is most commonly used to catch Carp?
11. Does the thickness of the ice impact your ability to catch fish?

Answers on page 161

Fish can get seasick too. Studies have found that when fish are kept aboard a rolling ship, they can get nauseous, just as same as humans. Aquarium fish on ships can exhibit anxiety on choppy seas, however, this is likely more due to water vibrations than visual confusion.

The only difference between a dreamer and a liar is the size of the fish.

# Pro Tip

When fishing for Salmon, make sure that your bait has something shiny on it to get the fish's attention. They like it when there isn't much light, so something that flashes in deeper, darker water often works well.

# Types Of Jigs

## SWIMMING JIGS

Swim jigging is the latest pro fishing technique. Swim jigging combines spinnerbait and jig movement to create a more realistic swim pattern.

A swimmer jig should weigh no more than half an ounce and have a bullet-shaped head for better glide. Swimming a jig requires landing it in a weedy or rocky strike zone and changing the retrieve speed. Avoid retrieving the jig too rapidly, since this raises it out of the bass strike zone.

## FLIPPING JIGS

Flipping jigs, often called Arkie jigs, are steady lures that won't catch on rocks or weeds, providing them more adaptability in shallow water. An enlarged hook, molded lead head, and weed guard make up a flipping jig. If you're fishing in a lead-free zone, try tungsten.

Flipping jigs exploit bass ambush tactics. Drop your jig in weeds or on a rock shelf. Keeping a little slack in the line, hop the jig along the bottom. This is a crawfish's protective motion, which rock bass eat.

# THE FOOTBALL JIG

Many anglers struggle to forecast post-summer bass activity and strike patterns. A football jig's distinctive construction makes it ideal for landing bass during this tough fishing season.

Football jigs have a tapered head and a light, thin hook that pierces the bass's mouth. Football-shaped head produces surprising yet steady movement on rocky ground. Dragging a jig across the water's bottom causes it to bounce like a walking crawfish.

Jigs are an all-season bass lure. With the perfect moves and patience, you'll score big.

Little Brooke always wondered what had happened in Big Cat's past life that he wouldn't talk about.

# GRANDPA KNOWS EVERYTHING ABOUT FISHING

# DIY Lures From Old Ammo

It is not difficult to fashion useful lures out of spent ammunition. Start by drilling a hole in the center of the shell. While working with centerfire cases, you can easily remove the primers; when working with rimfire cases, you can use a hammer and nail to punch a hole through the base of the case. Paint some colorful eye spots onto the case, and then thread it onto the line such that it wraps around a treble hook that has a yarn skirt. And bingo! You have a great homemade lure.

TRUE LOVE

# SIX steps to catching fish
## 1- cast
## 2- hook it
## 3- lose it
## 4- cuss and swear
## 5- cry like a baby
## 6- REPEAT

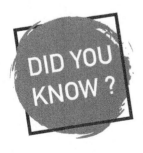

DID YOU KNOW ?

The majority of fish do not have eyelids.
Consider swimming all day while unable to blink.
A shark is the only fish that can blink.

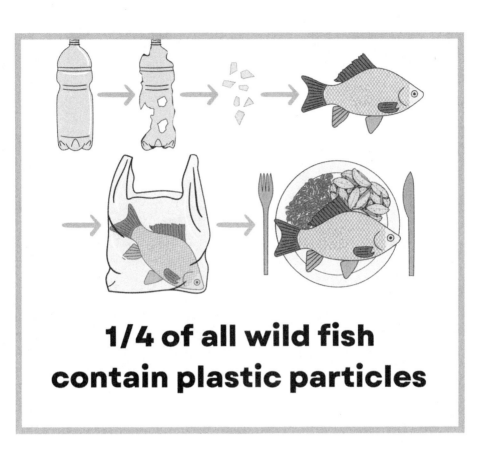

# 1/4 of all wild fish contain plastic particles

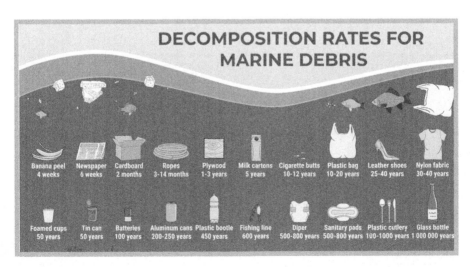

With his new rod and reel, and great weather, Davie was certain it was going to be a perfect day.

It was the first time Jimmy saw the little know Zombie fish

# Pro Tip

When fishing in waters where sharks are known to frequent, avoid wading in deeper water during early dawn or twilight (or later) since that is when sharks are most active and feeding.

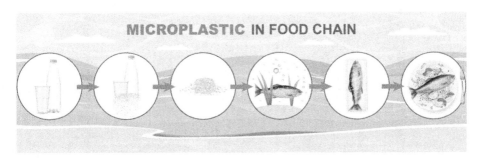

Plastic waste accounts for 80% of all marine pollution, with around 8 to 10 million metric tons of plastic ending up in the oceans each year. Always pick up your plastic so it doesn't pollute our water.

Little did Maurice know that little Minnow had a real badass big brother.

# TECHNIQUES FOR JIG FISHING EVERY ANGLER SHOULD KNOW

Although there are many different jigging techniques, mastering the fundamentals is essential for properly using jigs. Cast out your jig hook first, then wait for it to sink until it touches the bottom. If your rig is very sensitive, you should feel the spoon touch the sand. If not, count a few seconds to be sure the jig is in the right place.

After that, jerk the rod's tip up and let the jig drop back to the water's surface. Vary the direction of the rod movement as you do the action again.

Try rotating the rod tip upward and to the side or from side to side to imitate the swimming movements of crawfish and baitfish. Then, reel the line in gently to maintain tension in anticipation of a strike.

To land a fish, you must use more skilled jigging tactics, and some jigs are more suited for certain prey than others. Here are the top three jigs and tips on how to utilize each one to land your monster fish successfully.

**ALEVIN**

**FREE GERM**

**FRY**

# THE LIFE CIRCLE OF SALMON

**EGGS**

**WHITEBAIT**

**SPAWNING SALMON**

**SMOLT**

**ADULT SALMON**

# Pro Tip

Since salmon spend the majority of their lives in the ocean depths, they prefer darker water, so overcast days are the best times to fish. Cloudy or rainy weather, dawn or dusk are all the best times for catching river salmon.

"Climate change has allowed him to do his fishing inside the house."

I WANT A GOOD WOMAN WHO LOVES TO FISH, DIG WORMS, AND OWNS A BOAT--PREFERABLY A MASTERCRAFT WITH A MERC MOTOR.

## Fishhook Eye Injuries

Eye injuries with fishhooks are uncommon but not unheard of. They can result in blindness or other severe eye injuries when they do.

First and foremost, do not attempt to remove the hook yourself. Quick and professional ophthalmology care at an emergency room or other surgical center is needed to remove the fish hook. This is important to avoid complications and minimize the damage to the eye.

When the hook gets embedded, do the following, then seek immediate medical attention.

- Never attempt to remove a fish hook from an eye, eyelid, or area close to the eye.
- Do not press anything against the eye that may add any pressure to the eyeball.
- Use a metal patch, a cup, or even a paper cup to cover the eye. Covering the eye helps prevent the hook from moving.
- Take great care to avoid adding any pressure to either the hook or the eye.
- Cover the unharmed eye if you can. If the healthy eye is covered, the damaged eye will move less. This might stop the afflicted eye from suffering additional damage.

No matter what you do, some days the fish just won't bite.

NEVER MET A PERSON WHO CAN FISH
AND WORRY AT THE SAME TIME.

# *Pro Tip*

Here are 3 Tips that can help on days with the fish don't want to bite:

- Replace your lure. Give the fish something else to bite. Try a slower lure if yours moves quickly. Try a bigger lure if yours it too small. Or try a totally different lure or bait.
- Change your casting. The overhead cast is a classic technique, but it's not necessarily the best. Sidearm casts are just as adaptable and produce less splash, making them desirable in many scenarios.
- Get a fishing camera. The GoFish Cam shows where and how fish are swimming. Cast and reel to see the underwater action. Using GoFish Cam's Float Accessory is worth considering. Many people have found it to be a real solution.

# Fishing With Frog Lures

The design of frog-style baits makes them ideal for weed mats. The light, weedless frogs glide over the foliage instead of bogging down in the muck-like lures with exposed hooks.

The frog is another bait a lot of anglers employ for fishing in pond water and around places with brushy areas or places with low-hanging tree cover. This is one of the best topwater lures for fishing in weeds.

- Cross the weeds quickly. The most common and likely most annoying method of frog fishing is this one. When you skim the frog across matted foliage with steady rod twitches, bass will blow up on it, but the fish frequently miss the bait. If you skim the bait over the mat and then allow it to remain motionless in the mat's openings, your chances of getting a good hook set are increased.

- Highlight Weed Edges. Skim a frog across the weeds when fishing small patches of mats or lily pads, and keep working it in the same way once it slides into open water.

When your lure lands in open water, keep twitching your rod to make the frog's legs kick and thrust like real frog legs.

- Try using woody area targets. Beneath willows and cypress trees are other great places to throw frog bait. The buzz a buzz bait makes when it vibrates close to wood is similar to the frog wriggling quickly. However, the buoyant frog has a clear advantage over the buzzer because it may pause and wait for a strike as opposed to the buzzer, which must be kept going or it would sink.

- Color Options for Frog Fishing. For fishing in clear water on sunny days or in muddy water, use frogs with black or dark colors. Chartreuse and white are the ideal frog colors in clear or discolored water with gloomy skies.

- Picking the right equipment. With a 7'6" heavy action rod and a baitcasting reel loaded with 40-50 lb braided line, cast a frog when fishing in dense foliage. The majority of frog fishing applications call for a medium-heavy action casting rod with a quick tip. With each crank of a high-speed casting reel, more line is drawn in, helping to close the gap on long-distance hooksets that are common when frog fishing.

DON'T FEAR THE FISH REAPER

WE NEED MORE COWFISH BELL!

GIVE A MAN A FISH
YOU FEED HIM
FOR A DAY

TEACH A MAN TO FISH
AND HE HAS TO BUY

GRAPHITE RODS
REELS SPINNERBAITS
JIGS, CRANKBAITS
JERKBAITS, PLASTICS
FLIES, WADERS
A BOAT AND A TRUCK

# Wadder Safety

Fishing while wading is a well-liked method since it allows anglers to have a more personal encounter with their quarry. Here are a few wade fishing basics, regardless of whether you're in a calm stream, pond, lake, or river suitable for wading.

Wading safety ensures your safety in shallow and deep water. We'll help even the most seasoned fisherman stay safe. Here's how to test the water, identify risks, and wade safely.

Take your time entering the water. With little visibility under the water in most lakes and streams, rushing into the water nearly guarantees a slip and fall. Water entry requires caution.

Walking and casting is enticing but not a safe thing to do, especially if you are not experienced in waders. Casting while you are walking adds an unneeded risk of falling. Waders fill quickly with water, and if you are not properly prepared can drag you under the surface.

Even experienced anglers can lose their balance when walking and casting, especially in rough water.

Always plant your feet, then cast.

Wading fishing requires the same gear as other styles. Wading shoes with good traction treads or material is invaluable. Slick bottom shoes or flip-flops are never wise to wear in the water. You will often not see the slick mossy rock until you are already on top of it. It is at those times that you need good traction.

Some experienced anglers claim wade fishing gear isn't complete without a stick. This permits smooth navigation through thick sections and added stability when footing is difficult.

When wearing chest waders, a wader belt is extremely important. If you slip, the water will rush into the waders and pull you down. A wader belt can save your life if you fall in deep or fast-moving water.

Wader safety is a simple thing that often gets forgotten. But planning ahead and planning safe could well save your life.

Jim's wife actually believed him when he said that he would save money tying his own flies.

# A RECIPE THAT CATFISH LOVE

Here is a cheap bait that catches channel catfish better than practically anything. Buy some really cheap hot dogs (the cheaper, the better). Cube them. Put the chopped pieces into a zip-lock bag. Then add a couple of tablespoons of minced garlic and 2-3 teaspoons of unsweetened (note-unsweetened) strawberry Kool-Aid. Red food dye will also work in a pinch. Cover the concoction with water, then zip it closed, and leave the bag in a cool place overnight.

Garlic provides another flavor/scent trail to the hot dogs, which catfish adore for some reason. Kool-Aid gives franks a vivid crimson color that catfish equate with bloody wounds. This increases the bait's appeal. When you're ready to fish, put a hot dog on your hook, leaving the barb out, then cast.

# Fishing Knots

### PALOMAR KNOT
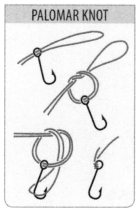

### EYE CROSSER KNOT
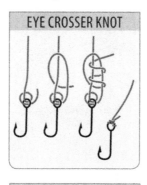

### DROPPER LOOP KNOT
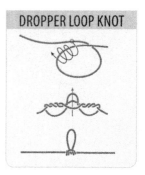

### IMPROVED CLINCH KNOT
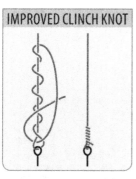

### WOLD'S FAIR KNOT

### SURGEON'S DROPPER KNOT
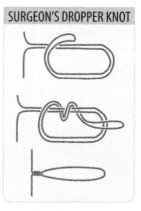

### STEPPED KNOT
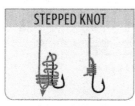

### NAIL KNOT

### BLOOD KNOT
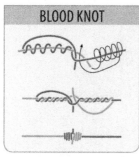

### NON-SLIP MONO KNOT
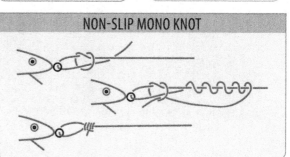

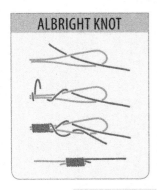

ALBRIGHT KNOT

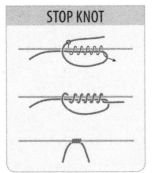

STOP KNOT

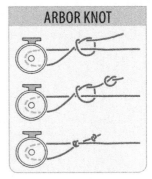

ARBOR KNOT

Lola the lonely mermaid finally
understood the humans' love of fishing.

# Cold Weather Bass Attack

As Autumn approaches, we hear that bass fishing will be abundant because fish have stocked up before their lengthy winter hibernation. Without a doubt, fishing is great in the fall, and huge fish certainly appear more active. However, this change is due to both the changing habitat and the migrations of the prey as well as the bass searching for their last meal in months.

The metabolic systems of fish adapt to temperature fluctuations to preserve life in the same settings they have evolved in since they are poikilothermic animals (who have blood the same temperature as the environment). The chemical balances and heart size of members of the sunfish family change physiologically to prepare them for cold. As lakes get closer to freezing, bass relative mobility decreases and digestion slows, but they still bite well in northern waters.

Large suckers and shiners placed on tip-ups are eaten by largemouth bass, who also hit lures jigged below a hole in the ice.

Many of the largest bass obtained each year in northeastern areas are caught through the ice.

Few North Country anglers fish for bass on frozen lakes, which may be advantageous for conservation. According to Roger Hugill, a fishery biologist with the Minnesota DNR, a group of ice anglers attempted to stop catch-and-release rules on a nearby lake. They contended that the greatest time to catch the juicy five-pound fish they liked to bake was during the winter.

According to physiological theories, bass only need to eat roughly a third as much food to stay nourished at 40 degrees as they do at 70. Winter also marks the lowest abundance of prey fish. But bass continue to eat.

Because key habitat is scarce in some systems, especially rivers, bass tend to be sedentary during the winter. However, underwater cameras in lakes and reservoirs show bass cruising in both shallow and deep waters, frequently coming closer to the camera for a better view.

# When Life Gives You Lemons

WHEN YOUR DAY GOES SIDEWAYS

AND EVERYTHING SUCKS...

THERE'S ALWAYS A SOLUTION TO MAKE LIFE RIGHT AGAIN.

# Rod Power and Action

If you've looked into new fishing rods, you've probably noticed that each rod's design specifications mention "Power" and "Action." Understanding these two elements is crucial since a rod's performance will vary greatly based on its power and action.

As you choose your next fishing rod, you can have a better understanding of these two design features.

## Rod Power

If you wish to cast weights for beach fishing or toss lures if you want a spinning rod, you need to take into account the "power" ratings used for fishing rods, which refer to the lifting capacity of each rod.

## Rod Action

Now that you understand what a fishing rod's "Power" is, we will explain what a fishing rod's "Action" is so you have all the information you need. Fishing rods can range in action from "Extra Fast" at one end of the scale to "Slow" at the other.

Since the bend on an Extra Fast action rod occurs just at the tip of the rod, setting the hook may be done more quickly because there is less of the rod to bend. Setting hooks are typically slower with a Slow rod since the bend extends much further down the rod, but these rods are perfect for activities like fly fishing where the extra bend is needed.

## Examples of Rod Power vs Action

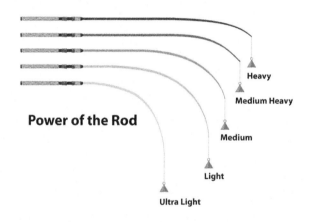

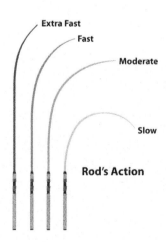

Always remember the #1 rule of fishing.
Fish come in three sizes.
Small, medium, and the
one that got away.

The proud dad!

There has been a lot of research done over the years to try and understand the mind of an avid fisher. There have been lots of theories, but as of yet, no one has been able to figure out what makes them tick. However, based on our wisdom and experience, we have come to our own conclusion as to why an angler's mind works as it does:

1. Because of all the time spent waiting and sitting on lakes or streams, their brains are free to wander aimlessly--and a wandering mind is a dangerous thing.
2. One's ability to stretch the truth expands proportionally to the number of beers consumed while fishing.
3. A fishing rod is the equivalent of a magic wand when it comes to coming up with their amazing tales.
4. A few too many synapses in my brain have been damaged due to prolonged exposure to the sun.
5. Last, but not least: they have paid far too much attention to what the fish have to say.

# MY DAD'S 5 RULES OF FISHING

1 - BAIT YOUR OWN HOOK
2 - CLEAN YOUR OWN FISH
3 - UNTANGLE YOUR OWN LINE
4 - DON'T FISH TOO CLOSE
5 - TELL YOUR OWN LIES

A fishing trip is when I sometimes get a buzz and sometimes catch a fish, but I always have a good time.

Sex is great while it lasts,
but fishing is great ALL day long.

# THE DEFINITION OF A CAMPING TRIP

When you spend a bunch of money and effort
to live like a homeless person.

## Decisions, Decisions...

Life is full of tough choices...
What the hell, I'll have both.

I'm a well-rounded person. There are lots of different things I do in my spare time.

I GO FISHING

RESEARCH FISHING

BUY FISHING GEAR

TALK ABOUT FISHING

DREAM ABOUT FISHING

# Have fun fishing

## EVEN WHEN YOU ARE TRAPPED AT HOME.

Naturally, fishing is best appreciated outside, but there are times when you are stuck at home and can't get out to your favorite lake, stream, or boating adventure. It's times like this that the world of video games come into play. A good fishing game can really make a bad day at home feel better.

There are some good, some bad, and some extremely bad fishing games out there. Virtual reality fishing simulations are the best. The majority of those can be found on apps and gaming consoles like the Nintendo Wii, where you can really use your hands to simulate casting and feel as though you're truly fishing.

While a realistic feel is important to the enjoyment of fishing games, the unrealistic aspect—catching fish ALL the time—is where the real fun lies. If you haven't yet tried some of these fishing games, it's worth a few minutes to check our 3 favorites:

 Bassmaster Fishing 2022: In this game, players can improve their fishing skills by taking part in both amateur and professional fishing tournaments. They can also get sponsors, upgrade their gear, and change the way their angler looks.

The game offers an Elite Tour, which has 8 different real-world locations where players can try to move up the ranks and become the Champion. It also has all-new multiplayer modes with beautiful environments and weather that changes.

The Catch: Carp & Coarse Fishing: A fishing game simulator with a slightly different take on the sport. In it, players can go to lakes, rivers, and oceans all over the world to try to catch more than 35 different kinds of fish and 125 "Boss Fish" ( the hardest fish in the game to catch).

The Catch has a lot of content for single players, but it also has a great multiplayer mode where players can compete online to see who can catch the most fish.

Fishing Sim World: Pro Tour: This game takes fishing as a sport to a whole new level. In it, players have to learn new things and improve their skills to catch rare fish and become the best anglers in the world. This means using the right tools and equipment for the catch and always being one step ahead of the competition. The game has both a single-player career mode and an online PvP mode where players can join online tournaments and make their own games with friends.

# Thank you!

# & Keep on Fishing!

Smilin'
Steve Lee

STEVE LOVES HAVING FUN. HIS MOTTO IS "FUNNY FIRST." HE WAS
RAISED BY A DAD WHO LOVED TO FISH AND A MOTHER WHOSE ONLY
FISHING RULE WAS, "IF YOU CATCH THEM, YOU CLEAN THEM: AND NOT IN
MY SINK."

DON'S NUMBER ONE GOAL IN BRINGING YOU THIS BOOK IS TO ADD A
LITTLE LAUGHTER TO YOUR LIFE.  HOPEFULLY, YOU'VE HAD SOME FUN.

# CHECK OUT THIS FUN-FILLED BOOK!

If you would like to enjoy some more humor and fun, please visit us here for fun free at:

ILoveGoodBooks.net/freestuff

# A FISHY QUIZ ANSWERS

1. What's the world's healthiest fish to eat?
   a. Alaskan salmon
2. What is the biggest fish in the world?
   a. Whale sharks
3. What is a lumpsucker?
   a. A fish
4. Some spearfishing masks have dark mirror glass. Why is this?
   a. The original idea of was to hide the human eyes from fish, It's controversial if it really works that good, but the amber ones do get you more vision in really murky water.
5. What are family groups of Dolphins called?
   a. A Pod
6. A soft-hackle nymph fly has just hooked one of the types of fish that are commonly caught using flies. What kind of fish would this be?
   a. Trout
7. What three types of fish have the fewest calories?
   Cod, flounder, and sole
8. What do you call a group of fish?
   School
9. What is jerkbait lure?
   Jerkbait is a minnow-shaped lure that implements a horizontal appearance when being reeled or pulled through the water.
10. What bait is most commonly used to catch Carp?
    Corn
11. Does the thickness of the ice impact your ability to catch fish?
    Yes

# References

Carlson, J. (2018, February 9). 11 Tips for River Safety | Friends of the River. Friends of the

River | The Voice of California's Rivers since 1973. Retrieved August 1, 2022, from

https://www.friendsoftheriver.org/2016/01/26/11-tips-for-river-safety/

Chauhan, A. (2020a, March 15). What To Know About Safe Wading Techniques.

OneAdventure. Retrieved August 1, 2022, from

https://www.oneadventure.com.au/safe-wading-techniques/

Chauhan, A. (2020b, March 15). What To Know About Safe Wading Techniques.

OneAdventure. Retrieved August 1, 2022, from

https://www.oneadventure.com.au/safe-wading-techniques/

Downs, A. (2020, February 20). How to Choose a Good Fishing Guide | MeatEater Fishing.

The Meat Eater. Retrieved August 1, 2022, from

https://www.themeateater.com/fish/general/how-to-choose-a-good-fishing-guide

Forde, B. (2021, June 8). 6 Frog Fishin&#039; Tips To Catch You More Bass. Karl's Fishing

Blog | Tips, Tricks & More | Karl's Bait & Tackle. Retrieved August 1, 2022, from

https://shopkarls.com/blog/6-frog-fishin-tips-to-catch-bass/

Healthwise Staff. (2021, July 1). First Aid for a Fish Hook Stuck in an Eye.

My Health Alberta Ca. Retrieved August 1, 2022, from

https://myhealth.alberta.ca/Health/aftercareinformation/pages/conditions.aspx hwid=aa113094&lang=en-ca

How to Catch Yellowfin Tuna - Tips for Fishing for Yellowfin Tuna. (n.d.).

How To Catch Any Fish. Retrieved August 1, 2022, from

https://www.howtocatchanyfish.com/yellowfin-tuna.html

How To Make Your Own Fishing Lures. (n.d.). Https://Www.Iwla.Org/. Retrieved August 1,

2022, from https://www.iwla.org/docs/default-source/outdoor-america-articles/how-to-make-your-own-fishing-lures.pdf?sfvrsn=423ca30d_2


J. (2018, June 17). How to Choose a Fly Rod. Telluride Angler. Retrieved August 1, 2022,

from https://tellurideangler.com/casting-pond/articles/how-to-choose-a-fly-rod/

Keith 'Catfish' Sutton, WorldFishingNetwork.com. (2019a, February 4). 10

Fishing Secrets You Don't Know About. Game & Fish. Retrieved August 1, 2022, from

https://www.gameandfishmag.com/editorial/10-fishing-secrets-you-dont-know-about/332031

Keith 'Catfish' Sutton,
WorldFishingNetwork.com. (2019b, February 4).

> 10 Fishing Secrets You Don't Know
> About. Game & Fish. Retrieved August 1,
> 2022, from

> https://www.gameandfishmag.com/editorial/10
> -fishing-secrets-you-dont-know-about/332031

Keith 'Catfish' Sutton,
WorldFishingNetwork.com. (2019c, February 4). 10

> Fishing Secrets You Don't Know About.
> Game & Fish.

> https://www.gameandfishmag.com/editorial/10
> -fishing-secrets-you-dont-know-about/332031

Kelley, M. (2020, November 23). Beginner's guide to
spearfishing techniques.

> Max Spearfishing. Retrieved August 1, 2022,
> from

> https://maxspearfishing.com/spearfishing-
> basics/beginners-guide-spearfishing-
> techniques

Morris, C. (2020, January 31).
Understanding Steelhead and How to Fly Fish For
Them

> [An Angler's Guide]. Flylords Mag - Flylords
> Mag. Retrieved August 1, 2022, from

> https://flylordsmag.com/steelhead-trout-
> oncorhynchus-mykiss-an-anglers-guide/

Nabreski, A. (2021, February 3). Ice Fishing Tips for Beginners. On The Water. Retrieved

August 1, 2022, from https://www.onthewater.com/how-to-ice-fish-for-beginners

Silverman, S., & Hughes, K. (2022, February 10). Best Trout Lures of 2022. Outdoor Life.

Retrieved August 1, 2022, from https://www.outdoorlife.com/gear/best-trout-lures/

Wired2fish. (2021, October 4). Fishing Rods: Understanding Lengths, Powers and Actions.

Retrieved August 1, 2022, from https://www.wired2fish.com/fishing-tips/fishing-rods-understanding-lengths-powers-and-actions#slide_3

# Annotations

123RF im: 120143963
©denizerkorkmaz

123RF Image ID:
12155595
©mammothis

123RF Image ID:
16493944
©toonerman

mage ID: 51229512
©grandslam

mage ID: 130011634
©lineartestpilot

123RF Image ID:
16482365
©toonerman

123RF Image ID:
52335334
©grandslam

123RF Image ID:
127692648
©edvard76

123RF Image ID:
180237586
©zdeneksasek

123RF Image ID:
108329795
©nataljacernecka

123RF Image ID:
139369991
©larryrains

mage ID: 9933135
©clairevFollow

123RF Image ID:
128160104
©mariafionawa

123RF Image ID:
31849129
©cteconsulting

123RF Image ID:
113560823
©john79

123RF Image ID:
34417955
©lolya1988

123RF Image ID:
60249745
©chudtsankov

123RF Image ID:
185299849
©littleprinceFollow

123RF Image ID:
123645940
©valeriikhadeiev

123RF Image ID:
28339883
©retroclipart

123RF Image ID:
117260506
©capeman29

123RF Image ID:
137155472
©tigatelu

123RF Image ID:
5901923
©izakowski

123RF Image ID:
14411431
©yurkina

123RF Image ID:
24336380
©tigatelu

123RF Image ID:
116615336
©derplan

123RF Image ID:
116615336
©derplan

123RF Image ID:
58794989
©kencor

123RF Image ID:
22777913
©stiven

123RF Image ID:
9611868
©ku2raza

123RF Image ID:
127906068
©afanasia

123RF Image ID:
168754700
©armi1961

123RF Image ID:
51871356
©jovanas

123RF Image ID:
90513140
©poemsuk

123RF Image ID:
101025596
©barbulat

123RF Image ID:
135070041
©robuart

123RF Image ID:
186782327
©ylivdesign

123RF Image ID:
49591232
©bronipoezd

123RF Image ID:
136862365
©zdeneksasek

123RF Image ID:
145425350
©arcady31

123RF Image ID:
89843347
©nora

123RF Image ID:
131223126
©studiobarcelona

123RF Image ID:
114844200
©zdeneksasek

123RF Image ID:
122944949
©studiostoks

123RF Image ID:
158501410
©ohmycut

123RF Image ID:
29381540
©majivecka

123RF Image ID:
98763151
©toricheks2016

123RF Image ID:
41250118
©kenbenner

123RF Image ID:
59489896
©fosgen

123RF Image ID:
161060463
©triptiart

123RF Image ID:
124018870
©blueasarisandi

123RF Image ID:
124018805
©blueasarisandiFollo
w

123RF Image ID:
161060466
©triptiart

123RF Image ID:
161060466
©triptiart

123RF Image ID:
154025927
©blueasarisandi

123RF Image ID:
44993309
©greatnotions

123RF Image ID:
123708972
©brillianata

123RF Image ID:
126724906
©platypusmi86

123RF Image ID:
3826046
©Suljo

123RF Image ID:
134077076
©ratselmeister

123RF Image ID:
134264277
©nataljacernecka

123RF Image ID:
124354555
©orensila

123RF Image ID:
68779874
©jianghaistudio

123RF Image ID:
111697339
©andrei45454

123RF Image ID:
171029546
©yaichatchai

123RF Image ID:
14656800
©1507kotl

123RF Image ID:
182286139
©gmast3r

123RF Image ID:
158998493
©aleksange

123RF Image ID:
77905341
©peterhermesfurianFo
llow

123RF Image ID:
162658503
©funny foryou

123RF Image ID:
127927794
©brgfx

123RF Image ID:
53298416
©bosecher

123RF Image ID:
42519985
©blueringmedia

123RF Image ID:
57011470
©sabelskayaFollow

123RF Image ID:
124539797
©guingmFollow

123RF Image ID:
16482185
©toonerman

123RF Image ID:
24082514
©andrewgenn

123RF Image ID:
46998579
©bosecher

123RF Image ID:
53300148
©bosecher

123RF Image ID:
123719733
©tigatelu

123RF Image ID:
170715331
©aleksangel

123RF Image ID:
176810956
©oleon17

mage ID: 17919882
©tribalium123

123RF Image ID:
162342718
©nataljacernecka

123RF Image ID:
124153121
©flobow

123RF Image ID:
51451594
©frescomovie

123RF Image ID:
130323831
©artistock

123RF Image ID:
61290211
©aleutie

123RF Image ID:
134017083
©kseniyshved

123RF Image ID:
137740734
©shock77

123RF Image ID:
181420966
©kseniyshved

123RF Image ID:
183688932
©arifulashif

123RF Image ID:
28465621
©denboma

123RF Image ID:
44329099
©iamcitrus

123RF Image ID:
124935598
©seamartini

123RF Image ID:
185961089
©seamartin

123RF Image ID:
128983104
©verzh

123RF Image ID:
26868351
©toonerman

123RF Image ID:
171038870
©dclipart

123RF Image ID:
19864919
©tigatelu

**Please check out all our books at**


ILoveGoodBooks.net

Printed in Great Britain
by Amazon

13856880R10099